Southern Living
LITTLE BOOK OF
Cheesecakes

Oxmoor
House

Cheesecake Bliss

Whether you're cooking for a holiday feast or simply have a hankering for the rich concoction, *Southern Living® Little Book of Cheesecakes* has a flavor for any mood or event. Cheesecakes are surprisingly simple to make and always impressive in presentation. They also hold up well and are ideal for freezing. They're a make-ahead dream dessert and the sweet tooth weakness of all ages.

We know that our readers have a real fondness for cheesecake by the number of recipes they send in for the creamy confection. The variety of cheesecakes attracts many aficionados. And opinions about the ideal cheesecake texture are almost as passionate as what constitutes great Southern barbecue. There are rich and creamy cheesecakes laced with whipping cream or sour cream, light and fluffy versions puffed up with egg whites, and dense, firm, and golden classics like New York-Style Cheesecake on page 8.

Cheesecakes can satisfy more than a sweet tooth. Try savory Sun-Dried Tomato Cheesecake on page 4 as a spread with crackers for a summer party that will leave guests clamoring for the recipe. Or sample the Italian flavors of Artichoke Cheesecake on page 6 sliced into wedges for a bridal luncheon.

Peruse our tips and hints and then start your baking exploration with Applause Cheesecake on page 40. With its pecan shortbread crust, creamy vanilla filling, and double toppings of chocolate and caramel, what's not to applaud?

Your Essential Cheesecake Tool

• **All you need is a springform pan**—a round pan with high, straight sides that clamp shut for baking and expand so you can remove the

cheesecake when the clamp is released.

• **Some people serve the cheesecake** on the bottom pan, but we like to carefully transfer the dessert to a serving plate if the crust is sturdy enough. A couple of large spatulas or one expandable spatula are handy for removing the bottom pan.

Quick Crust Solutions

Most cheesecake crusts start with crumbs of cookies or crackers, so crust flavors are as varied as the boxes on that aisle of the grocery store. Look under the "crusts" entry of our index on page 48 to peruse the options among these recipes. Pick your favorite flavor and use one of the four methods below for crumbs.

- **Give them a whirl:** If starting with whole cookies or crackers, pulse them in a food processor until crumbs form.

- **Blender basics:** You can use a blender instead of a food processor. Add cookies or crackers in smaller batches; make sure to pulse, not pulverize.

- **The old-fashioned way:** Place the cookies or crackers in a zip-top plastic bag; roll a heavy rolling pin or bottle gently over bag to make crumbs.

- **In a time crunch:** Buy boxed crumbs—the work's already done for you.

Making and Baking Hints

- **Let cream cheese soften** at room temperature before you begin.

- **Use shiny aluminum pans** for baking cheesecakes. If you already have a dark pan, decrease the baking time by 10 minutes.

- **When a cheesecake is done,** the center third of the cake should jiggle slightly. At this point, unless the recipe instructs you to turn the oven off and let the cheesecake cool in the oven, place the cheesecake on a wire rack and immediately run a knife around the edge of the cheesecake to release sides of pan. This allows the loosened sides to contract freely. Let the cheesecake cool completely to room temperature, and then cover and chill until ready to serve.

- **If your cheesecake cracks,** don't worry. Some cracking is normal during baking. As a rule, the slower the cheesecake is cooked, the less it will crack. To ensure that your cheesecake cooks slowly and evenly, use an oven thermometer to gauge the correct temperature. Another way to help prevent the cheesecake from cracking is to run a knife around the edge of the cake immediately after baking. Of course, there are creative ways to camouflage a cracked cake. Try using fruit or nut toppings or use the "tasteful" solution of sour cream topping from Deluxe Cheesecake on page 7.

- **If you're making the cheesecake ahead,** simply leave it in the pan after it has cooled, and cover and chill until serving time.

- **Cheesecakes can be frozen** up to one month. When the cheesecake is cooled completely, remove the pan, place the cheesecake on a cardboard circle, if desired, and wrap tightly in heavy-duty aluminum foil. Thaw the cheesecake in the refrigerator the day before serving.

Sun-Dried Tomato Cheesecake

Find edible flowers for garnish next to the fresh herbs in the produce section of larger grocery stores. We chose pansies, marigolds, and nasturtiums, but you can use your favorite edible flower.

½ cup minced dried tomatoes in oil
½ (15-ounce) package refrigerated piecrusts
1½ pounds dried beans (to use as pastry weights)
2 (8-ounce) packages cream cheese, softened
3 large eggs
1 (5-ounce) package shredded Swiss cheese

3 green onions, chopped (about ¼ cup)
½ teaspoon salt
½ teaspoon pepper
¼ teaspoon ground red pepper
1¾ cups sour cream
Garnishes: edible pansies, marigolds, and nasturtiums; fresh chives, green onion stems, fresh mint leaves

- Drain tomatoes well, pressing between paper towels. Set aside.
- Unfold piecrust. Press piecrust onto bottom and up sides of a 7-inch springform pan. Press out folds in piecrust on sides of pan; fold edges under and crimp. Freeze piecrust 30 minutes.
- Gently fit a 12-inch square of parchment paper over crust. Fill with 1½ pounds dried beans to weigh down parchment paper, filling to top edge of crust.
- Bake at 450° for 10 minutes. Remove piecrust from oven, and reduce oven temperature to 350°. Remove beans from parchment paper; let beans cool, and reserve beans for another use. Carefully remove parchment paper from crust.
- Beat cream cheese at medium speed with an electric mixer 2 to 3 minutes or until light and fluffy. Add eggs, 1 at a time, beating well after each addition. Stir in tomatoes, Swiss cheese, and next 4 ingredients, mixing well. Pour into baked piecrust.
- Bake on lower rack at 350° for 35 to 40 minutes or until golden brown and set. Cool slightly. Spread sour cream evenly over top. Cool cheesecake on a wire rack 20 minutes; cover and chill 8 hours. Place cheesecake on a serving plate; gently run a knife around edge of cheesecake to release sides of pan. Garnish, if desired. Serve with assorted crackers. Yield: 1 (7-inch) cheesecake.

Artichoke Cheesecake

Serve this dense, chunky cheesecake as a spread with crackers at a party or sliced into wedges for a luncheon.

¼ cup fine, dry breadcrumbs (store-bought)
¼ cup grated Parmesan cheese
2 tablespoons dried Italian seasoning
2 (8-ounce) packages cream cheese, softened
4 ounces crumbled feta cheese
3 large eggs
1 (8-ounce) container sour cream
1 (14-ounce) can artichoke hearts, drained and chopped

¾ cup chopped red bell pepper
¾ cup chopped green bell pepper
¾ cup chopped green onions (including ½-inch green tops)
1 large garlic clove, pressed
1 teaspoon dried tarragon
1 teaspoon dried basil

• Generously butter a 9-inch springform pan. Combine first 3 ingredients; sprinkle half of breadcrumb mixture on bottom of pan, and set aside remaining mixture.
• Position knife blade in a food processor bowl; add cream cheese. Process until smooth, stopping to scrape down sides. Add feta cheese, eggs, and sour cream. Process until smooth, stopping to scrape down sides. Add chopped artichoke and remaining 6 ingredients to processor. Process until smooth, stopping to scrape down sides. Pour mixture into prepared pan.
• Bake at 375° for 45 to 50 minutes or until golden. Cool completely in pan on a wire rack. Cover and chill at least 2 hours.
• Carefully remove sides of springform pan. Pat reserved breadcrumb mixture on sides of cheesecake. Serve with assorted crackers. Yield: 1 (9-inch) cheesecake.

Deluxe Cheesecake

If you've never made a cheesecake, this is a great basic recipe to use. It's a rich, dense cheesecake with a sour cream topping that hides any cracks or flaws in the cheesecake's top.

1 (5⅓-ounce) packet graham
    crackers, crushed (about
    1⅔ cups)
¼ cup sugar
6 tablespoons butter or
    margarine, melted
3 (8-ounce) packages cream
    cheese, softened

1 cup sugar
3 large eggs
½ teaspoon vanilla extract
1 (16-ounce) container sour
    cream
3 tablespoons sugar
½ teaspoon vanilla extract

● Combine graham cracker crumbs, ¼ cup sugar, and butter; mix well. Press graham cracker crust mixture into an ungreased 10-inch spring-form pan; set aside.
● Beat cream cheese at high speed with an electric mixer until creamy; gradually add 1 cup sugar, beating well. Add eggs, 1 at a time, beating after each addition. Stir in ½ teaspoon vanilla. Pour into prepared crust. Bake at 375° for 35 minutes or until cheesecake is set.
● Beat sour cream at medium speed 2 minutes. Add 3 tablespoons sugar and ½ teaspoon vanilla; beat 1 more minute. Spread over cheesecake. Bake at 400° for 5 minutes. Cool to room temperature on a wire rack; cover and chill 8 hours. Yield: 1 (10-inch) cheesecake.

New York-Style Cheesecake

This classic is a little denser than some cheesecakes.
It's great served with canned cherry pie filling or chopped fresh
strawberries and whipped cream—take your pick!

1 cup graham cracker crumbs
3 tablespoons butter, melted
2 tablespoons sugar
2 (8-ounce) packages cream
    cheese, softened
1 (3-ounce) package cream
    cheese, softened

½ cup sugar
1 tablespoon all-purpose flour
1½ teaspoons vanilla extract
1 large egg
½ cup sour cream
Garnish: cherry pie filling or
    chopped strawberries

• Stir together first 3 ingredients. Press crumb mixture onto bottom and 1½ inches up sides of a lightly greased 7-inch springform pan. Bake crust at 350° for 8 minutes. Cool on a wire rack.

• Beat cream cheese at medium speed with an electric mixer until smooth. Gradually add ½ cup sugar, flour, and vanilla, beating until blended. Add egg, beating until blended after each addition. Add sour cream, and beat just until blended. Pour mixture into prepared crust.

• Bake at 350° for 50 minutes or until center is almost set. Remove cheesecake from oven; cool on a wire rack. Cover and chill 8 hours. Gently run a knife around edge of cheesecake to release sides of pan; garnish, if desired. Yield: 1 (7-inch) cheesecake.

Bananas Foster Cheesecake

All the flavors of Bananas Foster, the quintessential New Orleans dessert, are incorporated in this creamy delight of a cheesecake.

¾ cup all-purpose flour
½ cup finely chopped pecans
¼ cup firmly packed brown sugar
¼ cup butter, melted and divided
2 teaspoons vanilla extract, divided
1 (8-ounce) package cream cheese, softened
1 (3-ounce) package cream cheese, softened
¾ cup granulated sugar
1 tablespoon cornstarch
2 large eggs

1 cup mashed very ripe banana (about 2 large)
1 (8-ounce) container sour cream, divided
2 teaspoons fresh lemon juice
1 teaspoon ground cinnamon
⅛ teaspoon salt
2 tablespoons granulated sugar
¼ teaspoon granulated sugar
¼ teaspoon ground cinnamon
1 ripe banana
¾ cup caramel topping
2 tablespoons dark rum

• Combine first 4 ingredients in a bowl; stir well. Stir in 1 teaspoon vanilla. Press pecan mixture onto bottom of a 7-inch springform pan; set aside.
• Beat cream cheese at medium speed with an electric mixer until creamy. Gradually add ¾ cup sugar and cornstarch, beating well. Add eggs, 1 at a time, beating after each addition. Stir in mashed banana, half the sour cream, lemon juice, remaining 1 teaspoon vanilla, 1 teaspoon cinnamon, and salt. Pour batter into prepared pan.
• Bake at 350° for 1 hour or until center is set. Remove from oven, and set aside.
• Combine remaining sour cream and 2 tablespoons sugar in a small bowl, stirring well. Spread over warm cheesecake; return to oven, and bake 10 more minutes. Cool on a wire rack. Cover and chill 8 hours.
• Gently run a knife around edge of cheesecake to release sides of pan; carefully remove sides of pan. Combine ¼ teaspoon sugar and ¼ teaspoon cinnamon in a small bowl; sprinkle over cheesecake. Peel and slice banana; arrange slices on top of cheesecake. Combine caramel sauce and rum in a small saucepan; cook over low heat until warm. Drizzle warm sauce over cheesecake, and serve with remaining sauce. Yield: 1 (7-inch) cheesecake.

Note: For testing purposes only, we used Smucker's caramel topping.

Pumpkin Cheesecake with Ginger Cream Topping

¾ cup granulated sugar, divided
¾ cup firmly packed brown
    sugar, divided
¾ cup graham cracker crumbs
½ cup finely chopped pecans
¼ cup butter or margarine,
    melted
1 tablespoon all-purpose flour
1½ teaspoons ground cinnamon
½ teaspoon ground ginger
½ teaspoon ground nutmeg
1 teaspoon vanilla extract
¼ teaspoon salt
1 (16-ounce) can pumpkin
3 (8-ounce) packages cream
    cheese, softened
3 large eggs
Ginger Cream Topping
Garnish: 16 pecan halves

• Combine ¼ cup sugar, ¼ cup brown sugar, graham cracker crumbs, ½ cup pecans, and butter; press into bottom and 1 inch up sides of a lightly greased 9-inch springform pan. Cover and chill 1 hour.
• Combine remaining ½ cup sugar, remaining ½ cup brown sugar, flour, and next 6 ingredients; set aside.
• Beat cream cheese at medium speed with an electric mixer until creamy. Add pumpkin mixture, beating well. Add eggs, 1 at a time, beating after each addition. Pour mixture into prepared crust. Bake at 350° for 55 minutes. Cool completely in pan on a wire rack.
• Spoon Ginger Cream Topping over cheesecake. Cover and chill at least 8 hours. To serve, carefully remove sides of pan; garnish cheesecake, if desired. Yield: 1 (9-inch) cheesecake.

Ginger Cream Topping

1 cup whipping cream
1 (8-ounce) container sour cream
2 tablespoons sugar
¼ cup minced crystallized ginger
3 tablespoons dark rum
½ teaspoon vanilla extract

• Combine first 3 ingredients in a bowl; beat at high speed with a mixer until soft peaks form. Fold in ginger, rum, and vanilla. Yield: 3 cups.

Praline-Crusted Cheesecake

2 cups crushed shortbread
  cookies
3 tablespoons butter or
  margarine, melted
4 Pralines, coarsely crumbled
5 (8-ounce) packages cream
  cheese, softened
1¾ cups sugar
2 tablespoons all-purpose flour

1½ teaspoons vanilla extract
4 large eggs
2 egg yolks
⅓ cup whipping cream
1 teaspoon grated lemon rind
2 (8-ounce) containers sour
  cream
⅓ cup sugar
Garnish: crumbled Pralines

• Combine cookie crumbs and butter. Press onto bottom and up sides of a greased 10-inch springform pan. Bake at 350° for 8 minutes. Cool on a wire rack. Sprinkle coarsely crumbled Pralines over crust.
• Beat cream cheese at medium speed with a heavy-duty electric mixer until creamy. Gradually add 1¾ cups sugar, flour, and vanilla, beating until smooth. Add eggs and egg yolks, 1 at a time, beating just until yellow disappears. Stir in whipping cream and lemon rind. Pour into crust. Place on a foil-lined baking sheet.
• Bake at 350° on lower oven rack 10 minutes. Reduce oven temperature to 325°; bake 1 hour and 20 minutes or until almost set. Cool on a wire rack 1 hour.
• Stir together sour cream and ⅓ cup sugar; spread over cheesecake.
• Bake at 325° for 10 minutes. Cool on a wire rack. Cover and chill 8 hours. Remove sides of pan. Garnish cheesecake, if desired. Yield: 1 (10-inch) cheesecake.

Pralines

Butter
¾ cup firmly packed light brown
  sugar
¾ cup granulated sugar
¾ cup half-and-half

3 tablespoons butter or
  margarine
1¼ cups coarsely chopped
  pecans
½ teaspoon vanilla extract

• Butter bottom of a heavy 3-quart saucepan. Cook brown sugar and next 3 ingredients in saucepan over low heat, stirring constantly, until sugars dissolve; stir in pecans. Bring to a boil over medium heat; cook, stirring occasionally, 6 to 8 minutes or until a candy thermometer registers 238° (soft ball stage). Remove from heat.
• Stir in vanilla; let stand 3 minutes. Beat with a wooden spoon 3 minutes or until mixture begins to thicken. Working rapidly, drop by tablespoonfuls onto wax paper. Let stand until firm. Yield: 1 dozen.

Cranberry Swirl Cheesecake

*Our Test Kitchens staff discovered that Pepperidge Farm Bordeaux
cookies make a great crumb crust.*

2¼ cups Bordeaux cookie
   crumbs
¼ cup butter or margarine,
   melted
1 (16-ounce) can whole-berry
   cranberry sauce
2 teaspoons ground cinnamon
¼ teaspoon ground cloves
3 (8-ounce) packages cream
   cheese, softened

1 cup sugar
1 tablespoon cornstarch
4 large eggs
1 teaspoon vanilla extract
Garnishes: sweetened whipped
   cream, fresh cranberries,
   fresh mint

• Combine cookie crumbs and melted butter; stir well. Press crumb
mixture onto bottom and 1 inch up sides of a lightly greased 9-inch
springform pan. Bake at 350° for 10 minutes. Let crust cool completely
on a wire rack.

• Position knife blade in a food processor bowl. Add cranberry sauce
and spices; process until smooth. Set aside.

• Beat cream cheese at medium speed with an electric mixer until
smooth. Add sugar and cornstarch; beat well. Add eggs, 1 at a time,
beating just until blended after each addition. Stir in vanilla.

• Pour half of batter into cookie crust; spoon ½ cup cranberry mixture
over batter. Swirl gently with a knife. Top with remaining batter. Spoon
½ cup cranberry mixture over cheesecake, and swirl gently with a
knife.

• Bake at 350° for 15 minutes. Reduce oven temperature to 225°. Bake
1 hour and 10 minutes.

• Remove from oven, and immediately run a knife around edge of
cheesecake to loosen it from pan. Turn oven off; return cheesecake to
oven, and cool in oven 1 hour. Remove from oven; cool completely in
pan on a wire rack. Chill, uncovered, until ready to serve. (Cheesecake
will continue to firm as it chills.)

• Carefully remove pan. Garnish, if desired. Serve cheesecake with
remaining cranberry mixture, if desired. Yield: 1 (9-inch) cheesecake.

Ambrosia Cheesecake

1½ cups almond shortbread
    cookie crumbs (about 12
    cookies)
3 tablespoons sugar
3 tablespoons butter or
    margarine, melted
4 (8-ounce) packages cream
    cheese, softened

3 large eggs
1 cup sugar
1 (14-ounce) package sweetened
    flaked coconut
2 teaspoons vanilla extract
2 cups Fresh Orange Curd
1 cup sweetened flaked coconut,
    lightly toasted (optional)

- Stir together first 3 ingredients; press mixture onto bottom of a 10-inch springform pan. Bake at 350° for 8 minutes. Cool.
- Beat cream cheese, eggs, and 1 cup sugar at medium speed with an electric mixer until fluffy. Stir in package of coconut and vanilla. Pour into prepared crust.
- Bake at 350° for 1 hour. Cool completely on a wire rack.
- Cover and chill 8 hours. Gently run a knife around edge of cheesecake to release sides of pan; carefully remove pan. Place cheesecake on a serving platter or cake stand. Spread Fresh Orange Curd evenly over top of cheesecake. Sprinkle 1 cup toasted coconut around outer edge of top, if desired. Yield: 1 (10-inch) cheesecake.

Note: For testing purposes only, we used Keebler Sandies Almond Shortbread.

Fresh Orange Curd

You can substitute reconstituted orange juice for fresh; however, squeezing navel oranges takes only about 15 minutes and can make all the difference in this cake's fresh flavor.

1 cup sugar
¼ cup cornstarch
2 cups fresh orange juice (about
    4 pounds navel oranges)

3 large eggs, lightly beaten
¼ cup butter
1 tablespoon grated orange rind

- Combine sugar and cornstarch in a 3-quart saucepan; gradually whisk in orange juice. Whisk in lightly beaten eggs. Bring to a boil (5 to 6 minutes) over medium heat, whisking constantly.
- Cook, whisking constantly, 1 to 2 minutes or until mixture reaches a puddinglike thickness. Remove from heat, and whisk in butter and orange rind. Cover, placing plastic wrap directly on curd, and chill 8 hours. Serve leftover sauce over ice cream or pound cake. Yield: about 3 cups.

Sweet Potato-Coconut Streusel Cheesecake

Write the name of this regal cheesecake on shimmery ribbon.

26 round buttery crackers, crumbled
¼ cup finely chopped pecans
¼ cup flaked coconut
3 tablespoons butter or margarine, melted
3 tablespoons all-purpose flour
1 tablespoon brown sugar
2 tablespoons butter or margarine
¼ cup flaked coconut
¼ cup pecan pieces

2 (8-ounce) packages cream cheese, softened
½ cup firmly packed light brown sugar
½ cup cooked, mashed sweet potato
¼ cup Kahlúa or other coffee liqueur
¼ teaspoon ground cinnamon
2 large eggs
Garnishes: sweetened whipped cream, ground cinnamon

• Combine first 4 ingredients; stir well. Firmly press crumb mixture onto bottom and 1 inch up sides of a 7-inch springform pan. Bake at 350° for 10 to 12 minutes. Remove to a wire rack; cool.
• Reduce oven temperature to 325°. Combine flour and 1 tablespoon brown sugar; cut in 2 tablespoons butter with a pastry blender until mixture is crumbly. Stir in ¼ cup coconut and ¼ cup pecan pieces. Set mixture aside. Cover and chill.
• Beat cream cheese at medium speed with an electric mixer until creamy; gradually add ½ cup brown sugar, beating well. Add sweet potato, Kahlúa, and ¼ teaspoon cinnamon; beat at low speed until blended. Add eggs, 1 at a time, beating after each addition. Pour batter into prepared crust.
• Bake at 325° for 50 minutes. Remove cheesecake from oven; sprinkle coconut mixture over top. Bake 25 more minutes. Let cheesecake cool to room temperature in pan on a wire rack. Cover and chill. To serve, gently run a knife around edge of cheesecake to release sides of pan; carefully remove pan. Garnish cheesecake, if desired. Yield: 1 (7-inch) cheesecake.

Note: Sprinkling cinnamon over two intricately shaped forks offers an appetizing invitation to enjoy a luscious slice.

Key Lime Cheesecake with Strawberry Sauce

Fresh Key lime juice makes this authentic,
but use bottled juice if fresh limes aren't available.

2 cups graham cracker crumbs
¼ cup sugar
½ cup butter or margarine,
    melted
3 (8-ounce) packages cream
    cheese, softened
1¼ cups sugar

3 large eggs
1 (8-ounce) container sour cream
1½ teaspoons grated lime rind
½ cup Key lime juice
Garnishes: strawberry halves,
    lime slices, lime zest
Strawberry Sauce

• Stir together first 3 ingredients, and firmly press into bottom and 1 inch up sides of a greased 9-inch springform pan. Bake at 350° for 8 minutes; cool.

• Beat cream cheese at medium speed with an electric mixer until fluffy; gradually add 1¼ cups sugar, beating until blended. Add eggs, 1 at a time, beating well after each addition. Stir in sour cream, rind, and juice. Pour batter into crust.

• Bake at 325° for 1 hour and 5 minutes; turn oven off. Partially open oven door; let cheesecake stand in oven 15 minutes. Remove from oven, and immediately run a knife around edge of cheesecake to release sides of pan.

• Cool completely in pan on a wire rack; cover and chill 8 hours. Garnish, if desired, and serve with Strawberry Sauce. Yield: 1 (9-inch) cheesecake.

Strawberry Sauce

1¼ cups fresh strawberries
¼ cup sugar

1½ teaspoons grated lime rind

• Process all ingredients in a food processor until smooth, stopping to scrape down sides. Yield: 1 cup.

Festive Piña Colada Cheesecake

6 tablespoons unsalted butter, melted
1¾ cups graham cracker crumbs
¾ cup chopped pecans, toasted
1 tablespoon sugar
3 (8-ounce) packages cream cheese, softened
½ cup sugar
5 large eggs
1 (8-ounce) can crushed pineapple, drained
1 cup cream of coconut
1 (8-ounce) container sour cream
⅓ cup light rum
4 teaspoons coconut extract
Glaze
Garnishes: whipped cream, toasted coconut

• Stir together first 4 ingredients, and press into bottom and 1½ inches up sides of a lightly greased 10-inch springform pan.
• Beat cream cheese and ½ cup sugar at medium speed with an electric mixer 3 minutes or until fluffy. Add eggs, 1 at a time, beating well after each addition. Add pineapple and next 4 ingredients, beating until blended. Pour mixture into crust.
• Bake at 325° for 1 hour and 15 minutes or until center is almost set. Cool on a wire rack. Spread Glaze over top of cheesecake. Cover and chill at least 8 hours. Garnish, if desired. Yield: 1 (10-inch) cheesecake.

Glaze

1 tablespoon cornstarch
1 tablespoon water
1 (8-ounce) can crushed pineapple, undrained
¼ cup sugar
2 tablespoons lemon juice

• Stir together cornstarch and 1 tablespoon water until smooth. Combine cornstarch mixture, crushed pineapple, ¼ cup sugar, and lemon juice in a saucepan over medium heat; cook, stirring constantly, 5 minutes or until mixture is thickened and bubbly. Remove from heat; cool completely. Yield: 1 cup.

Jeweled Cheesecake

2¼ cups gingersnap cookie
   crumbs
6 tablespoons butter or
   margarine, melted
⅔ cup whipping cream
1 pound white chocolate, finely
   chopped

4 (8-ounce) packages cream
   cheese, softened
1 cup sugar
6 large eggs
1 teaspoon vanilla extract
Candied Cranberries (optional)
Pistachio Crunch (optional)

• Combine gingersnap crumbs and melted butter; stir well. Press crumb mixture into bottom and 1 inch up sides of a 10-inch spring-form pan. Bake at 350° for 10 minutes. Cool.

• Reduce oven temperature to 300°. Bring whipping cream to a simmer in a saucepan. Remove from heat, and pour over chocolate in a large bowl. Stir mixture with a rubber spatula until smooth. Cool.

• Beat cream cheese at high speed with an electric mixer until creamy. Add sugar; beat well. Add eggs, 1 at a time, beating after each

addition. Fold in chocolate mixture. Stir in vanilla. Pour batter into prepared crust.
- Bake at 300° for 1 hour and 15 minutes. Cool completely on a wire rack. Cover and chill at least 8 hours. Gently run a knife around edge of cheesecake to release sides of pan; carefully remove pan. If desired, decorate cheesecake with Candied Cranberries and Pistachio Crunch. Yield: 1 (10-inch) cheesecake.

Candied Cranberries

2½ cups sugar
1 cup hot water
¾ cup cranberry-apple juice
    drink

3½ cups fresh cranberries

- Combine first 3 ingredients in a small nonaluminum saucepan. Bring to a boil; reduce heat, and simmer, uncovered, until sugar dissolves, stirring occasionally.
- Remove from heat, and pour syrup mixture over cranberries in a medium-size heatproof bowl. Place bowl on a steamer rack in a large Dutch oven over simmering water. Cover and steam 30 minutes. Remove bowl of cranberries. Cool completely without stirring.
- Cover bowl with cheesecloth; let stand at room temperature for 3 days, stirring occasionally. (Mixture will become thick.)
- Transfer cranberries, using a slotted spoon, to a large mesh wire rack placed over a wax paper-lined jellyroll pan. Store cranberry syrup in a glass container in refrigerator for another use. Let fruit dry, uncovered, for 2 to 3 days, turning occasionally. Reserve ¼ cup Candied Cranberries for use in Pistachio Crunch. Yield: 2½ cups candied cranberries and 2 cups syrup.

Note: Candied Cranberries can be prepared and refrigerated up to 1 week ahead.

Pistachio Crunch

12 ounces vanilla bark coating
⅓ cup chopped, toasted
    pistachio nuts

¼ cup Candied Cranberries,
    chopped

- Melt candy coating in a heavy saucepan over low heat, stirring constantly. Remove from heat.
- Stir in nuts and cranberries. Spread mixture in a thick layer (about ¼ inch) on a wax paper-lined baking sheet. Cool completely. Break into pieces or use Christmas cookie cutters to cut desired shapes. Yield: 1 pound.

Fresh 'n' Healthy Lemon-Berry Cheesecake

¾ cup crushed gingersnap
   cookies
3 tablespoons quick-cooking
   oats, uncooked
2 tablespoons butter, melted
Vegetable cooking spray
1 (16-ounce) container 1% low-fat
   cottage cheese
1 (8-ounce) package ⅓-less-fat
   cream cheese, softened

⅔ cup sugar
3 tablespoons all-purpose flour
1 teaspoon grated lemon rind
   (about 1 lemon)
2 tablespoons fresh lemon juice
   (about 1 lemon)
2 large eggs
1 large egg white
1 teaspoon vanilla extract
2 cups raspberries

• Place crushed gingersnaps, oats, and butter in a food processor; process until blended. Press into bottom and 1 inch up sides of a 7-inch springform pan coated with cooking spray. Bake at 350° for 6 minutes. Remove from oven; cool completely.
• Reduce oven temperature to 325°. Combine cottage cheese and cream cheese in a food processor; process 2 minutes or until smooth. Add sugar and next 6 ingredients; process 1 minute or just until blended. Pour cheese mixture over prepared crust.
• Bake at 325° for 1 hour and 5 minutes or until center is almost set (center will be soft but will firm when chilled). Turn off oven; leave cheesecake in oven 30 minutes. Remove cheesecake from oven; gently run a knife around edge of cheesecake to release sides of pan. Cool to room temperature on a wire rack. Cover and chill 8 hours.
• Unmold cheesecake onto a serving platter. Serve with raspberries. Yield: 1 (7-inch) cheesecake (serving size: ¹⁄₁₀ cheesecake).

Per serving: Calories: 284 (41% from fat); Fat: 13.2g (sat 7.1g, mono 4.4g, poly 0.8g); Protein 11g; Carb 32g; Fiber 2.1g; Chol 75mg; Iron 1.7mg; Sodium 374mg; Calc 70mg

Low-Fat Cheesecake with Cherry Topping

¾ cup graham cracker crumbs
¼ cup sugar
2 tablespoons butter, melted
2 teaspoons water
Vegetable cooking spray
3 (8-ounce) packages fat-free
    cream cheese, softened
2 (8-ounce) packages ⅓-less-fat
    cream cheese, softened
1 cup sugar
3 tablespoons all-purpose
    flour
¼ teaspoon salt

1 (8-ounce) container fat-free
    sour cream
4 large eggs
2 teaspoons vanilla extract
1 vanilla bean, split lengthwise
⅔ cup tawny port or other sweet
    red wine
½ cup sugar
2 (10-ounce) bags frozen pitted
    dark sweet cherries
2 tablespoons fresh lemon juice
4 teaspoons cornstarch
4 teaspoons water

• Combine first 3 ingredients, tossing with a fork. Add 2 teaspoons water; toss with a fork until moist and crumbly. Gently press mixture into bottom and 1½ inches up sides of a 9-inch springform pan coated with cooking spray. Bake at 400° for 5 minutes; cool on a wire rack.
• Reduce oven temperature to 325°.
• Beat cheeses at high speed with an electric mixer until smooth. Combine 1 cup sugar, flour, and salt, stirring with a whisk. Add to cheese mixture; beat well. Add sour cream; beat well. Add eggs, 1 at a time, beating well after each addition. Stir in vanilla extract. Scrape seeds from vanilla bean; stir seeds into cheese mixture, reserving bean halves.
• Pour cheese mixture into prepared pan; bake at 325° for 1 hour and 15 minutes or until cheesecake center barely moves when pan is touched. Remove cheesecake from oven; gently run a knife around edge of cheesecake to release sides of pan. Cool to room temperature. Cover and chill at least 8 hours.
• To prepare topping, combine port, ½ cup sugar, cherries, and reserved vanilla bean halves in a large saucepan; bring to a boil. Cook 5 minutes or until cherries are thawed and mixture is syrupy. Remove vanilla bean halves; discard.
• Combine juice, cornstarch, and 4 teaspoons water, stirring with a whisk until well blended. Stir cornstarch mixture into cherry mixture; bring to a boil. Reduce heat; simmer 3 minutes or until mixture is slightly thickened and shiny. Remove from heat; cool to room temperature. Cover and chill. Serve over cheesecake. Yield: 1 (9-inch) cheesecake (serving size: 1/16 cheesecake and 2 tablespoons sauce).

Per serving: Calories: 305 (29% from fat); Fat: 9.7g (sat 1.1g, mono 1.2g, poly 0.4g); Protein 12g; Fiber 1.9g; Carb 40g; Chol 85mg; Iron 0.9mg; Sodium 538mg; Calc 251mg

Frozen Peppermint Cheesecake

Crushed peppermint candy imbues this no-bake cheesecake with holiday spirit. For a classic pairing, serve slices afloat in rich chocolate sauce.

1¼ cups chocolate wafer crumbs
  (about 25 wafers)
¼ cup sugar
¼ cup butter or margarine,
  melted
1 (8-ounce) package cream
  cheese, softened

1 (14-ounce) can sweetened
  condensed milk
1 cup crushed hard peppermint
  candy
2 cups whipping cream

• Stir together first 3 ingredients; press into bottom and 1 inch up sides of a 9-inch springform pan. Set aside.
• Beat cream cheese at medium speed with an electric mixer until creamy. Gradually add condensed milk, beating until smooth. Stir in candy.
• Beat whipping cream until soft peaks form; gently fold whipped cream into cream cheese mixture. Pour into prepared pan. Cover and freeze 6 hours or until firm. Gently run a knife around edge of cheesecake to release sides of pan; carefully remove pan just before serving. Yield: 1 (9-inch) cheesecake.

Frozen Pistachio Cheesecake

Two things distinguish this velvety cheesecake: It's frozen, rather than baked (except for the crust), and it's made without eggs.

½ cup pistachio nuts
1 cup brown edge wafer
   cookie crumbs
1½ tablespoons granulated sugar
¼ cup butter or margarine, melted
½ cup whipping cream
6 ounces white chocolate, finely
   chopped

2 (8-ounce) packages cream
   cheese, softened
⅓ cup butter or margarine,
   softened
⅓ cup sifted powdered sugar
1 teaspoons vanilla extract
Garnish: additional pistachio
   nuts

- Position knife blade in food processor bowl; add ½ cup pistachio nuts. Process until chopped. Add wafer cookie crumbs, 1½ tablespoons sugar, and melted butter. Pulse 4 or 5 times or until blended. Press crumb mixture onto bottom and 1½ inch up sides of a lightly greased 7-inch springform pan. Bake at 350° for 12 minutes or until lightly browned. Cool completely on a wire rack.
- Bring whipping cream to a simmer in a heavy saucepan over medium heat. Remove from heat, and add chopped white chocolate. Let stand 2 to 3 minutes. Stir gently with a rubber spatula until smooth.
- Beat cream cheese and softened butter at medium speed of an electric mixer until creamy. Add powdered sugar, and beat until light and fluffy. Add melted white chocolate mixture and vanilla; beat 3 minutes or until very smooth. Pour batter into prepared crust. Cover and freeze at least 8 hours or up to 1 month.
- Let stand at room temperature about 30 minutes before serving. Gently run a knife around edge of cheesecake to release sides of pan; carefully remove pan. Garnish cheesecake, if desired. Cut frozen cheesecake with a sharp knife, dipping knife in hot water and wiping it dry between each slice. Yield: 1 (7-inch) cheesecake.

Note: For testing purposes only, we used Pepperidge Farm Chessmen butter cookies and Nestlé white chocolate.

Tipsy Eggnog Cheesecake

You can store Sugared Rose Petals in an airtight container several months.

2 cups wheatmeal biscuit crumbs
⅓ cup butter or margarine,
    melted
2 tablespoons sugar
½ teaspoon ground nutmeg
3 (8-ounce) packages cream
    cheese, softened
1 cup sugar

1 tablespoon cornstarch
5 large eggs
¾ cup canned or homemade
    eggnog
¼ cup dark rum
¼ cup brandy
Sugared Rose Petals (optional)

- Combine first 4 ingredients; stir well. Firmly press crumb mixture into bottom and 1½ inches up sides of a lightly greased 9-inch spring-form pan. Bake at 325° for 12 to 15 minutes. Remove to a wire rack; cool.
- Beat cream cheese at medium speed with an electric mixer until creamy; gradually add 1 cup sugar and cornstarch, beating well. Add eggs, 1 at a time, beating after each addition. Stir in eggnog, rum, and brandy. Pour batter into prepared crust.
- Bake at 325° for 1 hour. (Center will be soft.) Remove from oven, and gently run a knife around edge of pan to release cheesecake from sides; return to oven. Turn oven off; leave cheesecake in oven, with oven door partially opened, 30 minutes. Cool to room temperature in pan on a wire rack. Cover and chill 8 hours.
- Gently run a knife around edge of cheesecake to release sides of pan; carefully remove pan, and top cheesecake with Sugared Rose Petals, if desired. Yield: 1 (9-inch) cheesecake.

Sugared Rose Petals

3 large pesticide-free roses
¼ cup frozen egg substitute,
    thawed and lightly beaten

½ cup superfine sugar

- Pull the petals free from 1 rose. Lightly coat each petal on both sides with egg substitute, using a small paintbrush.
- Sift a small amount of sugar over the coated petals, turning them carefully to coat both sides. Set on wax paper to dry at least 1 hour. Repeat procedure with remaining roses, egg substitute, and sugar. Yield: 1½ cups.

Note: Substitute other edible flowers, if desired. Many grocery stores carry prepackaged edible flowers.

Low-fat Orange-Glazed Cheesecake with Gingersnap Crust

1 cup gingersnap crumbs
2 tablespoons sugar
1 tablespoon butter, melted
Vegetable cooking spray
2 (8-ounce) packages fat-free
    cream cheese, softened
2 (8-ounce) packages ⅓-less-fat
    cream cheese, softened
1 (8-ounce) container reduced-fat
    sour cream
¼ cup all-purpose flour
1½ cups sugar
¼ cup thawed orange juice
    concentrate, undiluted

1 tablespoon Grand Marnier or
    other orange liqueur or
    orange juice concentrate
2 teaspoons vanilla extract
3 large eggs
2 large egg whites
½ cup orange marmalade
1 tablespoon Grand Marnier or
    other orange liqueur or
    orange juice concentrate
1 orange, peeled and sliced

• Combine first 3 ingredients; toss with a fork until moist. Press into bottom of a 9-inch springform pan coated with cooking spray. Bake at 325° for 5 minutes.
• Beat cheeses and sour cream in a large bowl at high speed with an electric mixer until smooth. Add flour, sugar, and next 3 ingredients, and beat well. Add eggs and egg whites, 1 at a time, beating well after each addition.
• Pour cheese mixture into prepared pan; bake at 325° for 1 hour and 10 minutes or until almost set. (Cheesecake is done when center barely moves when pan is touched.) Remove cheesecake from oven; gently run a knife around the edge of cheesecake to release sides of pan. Cool to room temperature. Carefully remove sides of pan.
• To prepare the topping, combine marmalade and 1 tablespoon liqueur. Spread half of mixture over top of cheesecake. Cut the orange slices in half, and arrange over cheesecake. Spread with remaining marmalade mixture. Cover and chill at least 8 hours. Yield: 1 (9-inch) cheesecake.

Per serving: Calories: 303 (31% from fat); Fat: 10.6g (sat 2.1g, mono 1.7g, poly 0.4g); Protein 11g; Carb 42g; Fiber 0.6g; Chol 71mg; Iron 0.9mg; Sodium 442mg; Calc 191mg

Crème de Cassis Cheesecake

1 cup vanilla wafer or butter
    cookie crumbs
2 tablespoons sugar
1 (2-ounce) square white
    chocolate, grated
¼ cup butter or margarine,
    melted
2 (8-ounce) packages cream
    cheese, softened
¾ cup sugar

2 tablespoons crème de cassis
⅛ teaspoon salt
2 large eggs
1 (2-ounce) square white
    chocolate, finely chopped
1 (8-ounce) container sour cream
2 tablespoons sugar
½ teaspoon almond extract
Garnish: white chocolate
    shavings

• Combine first 4 ingredients; press into bottom and up sides of a 7-inch springform pan. Chill.

• Beat cream cheese and ¾ cup sugar at high speed with an electric mixer until light and fluffy. Add crème de cassis and salt; mix well. Add eggs, 1 at a time, beating just until blended after each addition. Fold in chopped chocolate. Pour batter into prepared pan. Place pan on a baking sheet. Bake at 350° for 50 to 52 minutes. Cool 10 minutes.

• Combine sour cream, 2 tablespoons sugar, and almond extract. Spread over cheesecake. Bake at 350° for 10 minutes. Cool on a wire rack. Refrigerate cheesecake at least 8 hours. Garnish, if desired. Yield: 1 (7-inch) cheesecake.

Cheesecake Sampler

This rich, dense New York-style cheesecake received our Test Kitchens highest rating—even without any toppings. Pick from one or all of our toppings that follow the main recipe.

2 cups graham cracker crumbs
½ cup butter or margarine,
    melted
2 tablespoons sugar
4 (8-ounce) packages cream
    cheese, softened

1¾ cups sugar
7 large eggs .
3 (8-ounce) containers sour
    cream
1 tablespoon vanilla extract
Cheesecake Toppings

- Combine first 3 ingredients; stir well. Press mixture firmly into bottom and up sides of a lightly greased 9-inch springform pan. Chill thoroughly.
- Beat cream cheese at high speed with a heavy-duty electric mixer until fluffy. Gradually add 1¾ cups sugar, beating well. Add eggs, 1 at a time, beating well after each addition. Add sour cream and vanilla; beat at low speed until smooth. Pour into prepared pan. Bake at 300° for 1 hour and 25 minutes. Turn off oven, and leave cheesecake in oven 4 hours. (Do not open oven door.)
- Remove cheesecake from oven; cool completely on a wire rack. Cover and chill 8 hours. Gently run a knife around edge of cheesecake to release sides of pan; carefully remove pan; transfer cheesecake to a serving platter. Cut into 8 wedges; top each slice with desired Cheesecake Toppings. Yield: 1 (9-inch) cheesecake.

Cheesecake Toppings

Orange Cheesecake: Brush orange marmalade evenly over slice. Cut candied orange slices in halves, thirds, and quarters. Arrange orange segments over slice.

Chocolate Lattice Cheesecake: Spoon 1 can each ready-made chocolate and cream cheese frostings into separate microwave-safe bowls. Microwave each at HIGH 20 seconds or just until soft and pipeable. Spoon frostings into separate zip-top freezer bags. Seal; snip a tiny hole in the corner of each bag. Pipe chocolate frosting in a zigzag fashion over the slice. Pipe cream cheese frosting over chocolate frosting in the opposite direction. Pipe additional chocolate frosting over cream cheese frosting. Place chocolate-covered coffee beans on crust edge, using chocolate frosting to secure in place.

Coconut Cheesecake: Spoon 1 can ready-made cream cheese frosting into a microwave-safe bowl. Microwave on HIGH 40 seconds or until melted and pourable. Pour over slice; sprinkle with grated fresh or frozen coconut.

Walnut Cheesecake: Spoon walnuts-in-syrup ice cream topping (such as Smucker's Walnuts in Syrup ice cream topping) over slice.

Peppermint Cheesecake: Spoon I can ready-made cream cheese frosting into a microwave-safe bowl. Microwave at HIGH for 30 seconds or until almost melted and stirring consistency. Combine frosting and crushed peppermint candy; stir well. Spread over slice. Place whole pillow-shaped peppermint candies around crust edge.

Raspberry Cheesecake: Brush melted seedless raspberry jam over slice. Arrange fresh raspberries over slice; brush lightly with additional melted jam.

Cinnamon Sensation Cheesecake: Spoon sweetened whipped cream or thawed frozen whipped topping into a decorating bag fitted with a large star tip. Pipe rosettes over slice, and sprinkle evenly with ground cinnamon. Place a pirouline cookie on the crust edge of slice.

Holly Cheesecake: Pipe green cake decorating gel in shape of holly leaves over slice. Arrange 3 red candy-coated chocolate-covered peanuts at top of leaves.

Chocolate-Mint Cheesecake

1 cup chocolate wafer crumbs
  (19 wafers)
2 tablespoons sugar
3 tablespoons butter or
  margarine, melted
1 cup (6-ounce package) semisweet chocolate morsels
1 teaspoon peppermint extract

3 (8-ounce) packages cream
  cheese, softened
⅔ cup sugar
3 large eggs
1 teaspoon vanilla extract
3 egg whites
1 (7-ounce) jar marshmallow
  cream

- Combine first 3 ingredients; press into bottom of a 7-inch spring-form pan. Bake at 350° for 10 minutes. Set aside.
- Melt chocolate morsels in a small heavy saucepan over low heat, stirring constantly. Stir in 1 teaspoon peppermint extract; set aside.
- Beat cream cheese at medium speed with an electric mixer until creamy; gradually add ⅔ cup sugar, beating well. Add eggs, 1 at a time, beating after each addition. Stir in melted chocolate and vanilla. Pour into prepared pan.
- Bake at 350° for 50 minutes.
- Remove from oven; gently run a knife around edge of pan to release sides, and cool completely in pan on a wire rack.
- Cover and chill 8 hours.
- Beat egg whites at high speed with an electric mixer until soft peaks form. Gradually add marshmallow cream; beat until stiff peaks form. Gently run a knife around edge of cheesecake to release sides of pan; carefully remove pan. Place cheesecake on a baking sheet. Carefully spread egg white mixture over top and sides of cake.
- Bake at 325° for 25 to 30 minutes or until golden. Serve immediately. Yield: 1 (7-inch) cheesecake.

Chocolate-Wrapped Banana Cheesecake

2 cups graham cracker crumbs
1 cup finely chopped dry-roasted
  peanuts
½ cup sugar
½ cup butter or margarine,
  melted
3 medium-size ripe bananas
2 teaspoons lemon juice
2 (8-ounce) packages cream
  cheese, softened

1 cup sugar
1 cup mascarpone cheese*
4 large eggs
1 tablespoon vanilla extract
1 cup milk chocolate morsels
1 tablespoon butter or margarine
Caramelized Bananas

• Stir together graham cracker crumbs, peanuts, ½ cup sugar, and ½ cup butter; press into bottom and 1 inch up sides of a 9-inch spring-form pan. Bake at 375° for 10 to 12 minutes. Cool on a wire rack.
• Mash bananas with a fork; stir in lemon juice until blended. Beat cream cheese and 1 cup sugar at medium speed with an electric mixer until light and fluffy. Add mascarpone, beating until smooth. Add eggs, 1 at a time, beating well after each addition. Stir in banana and vanilla. Pour into prepared crust.
• Bake at 325° for 1 hour (center will be slightly soft). Remove from oven; gently run a knife around edge of pan to loosen sides. Cool on a wire rack; cover and chill 8 hours.
• Microwave chocolate and butter in a 1-quart microwave-safe bowl at HIGH 60 seconds; stir until smooth. Let stand 30 minutes.
• Gently run a knife around edge of cheesecake to release sides of pan; carefully remove sides of pan. Spread three-fourths of melted chocolate around sides of cheesecake. Arrange Caramelized Bananas on top; drizzle with remaining chocolate. Yield: 1 (9-inch) cheesecake.

*Substitute 1 (8-ounce) package cream cheese, 2½ tablespoons sour cream, and 2 tablespoons whipping cream for mascarpone cheese. Beat ingredients well at medium speed with an electric mixer. Use 1 cup mixture for cheesecake recipe, reserving remainder for other uses.

Caramelized Bananas

4 medium bananas
½ cup firmly packed light brown
  sugar

¼ cup butter or margarine

• Cut bananas diagonally into ⅓-inch-thick slices.
• Cook brown sugar and butter over high heat in a small skillet, stirring constantly, 5 minutes or until thickened. Remove from heat; stir in banana. Cool. Yield: 1¼ cups.

Turtle Cheesecake

For those who love turtle candies, here's the cheesecake version.

2 cups chocolate wafer crumbs
    (38 wafers)
¼ cup sugar
⅓ cup butter, melted
3 (8-ounce) packages cream
    cheese, softened
1¼ cups sugar
4 large eggs

1 (8-ounce) container sour cream
1 tablespoon vanilla extract
¼ cup butter
1 cup (6-ounce package)
    semisweet chocolate
    morsels
1 (12-ounce) jar caramel topping
1 cup chopped pecans

- Combine first 3 ingredients; stir well. Firmly press mixture into bottom and 1 inch up sides of a lightly greased 9-inch springform pan. Bake at 325° for 10 minutes. Cool in pan on a wire rack.
- Beat cream cheese at medium speed with an electric mixer until creamy; gradually add 1¼ cups sugar, beating well. Add eggs, 1 at a time, beating after each addition and scraping sides and bottom as needed. Stir in sour cream and vanilla. Pour batter into prepared crust.
- Bake at 325° for 1 hour and 5 minutes. (Center will not be completely set.) Turn oven off, and partially open oven door; leave cake in oven 1 hour. Cool completely on a wire rack; cover and chill at least 8 hours. Gently run a knife around edge of cheesecake to release sides of pan; carefully remove pan. Transfer cheesecake to a serving plate.
- Melt ¼ cup butter in a small heavy saucepan; add chocolate morsels. Stir over low heat just until chocolate melts and mixture blends. Spread warm chocolate mixture over cheesecake; chill 15 minutes.
- Combine caramel topping and pecans in a small saucepan. Bring to a boil, stirring constantly, over medium heat; boil 2 minutes. Remove from heat, and cool 5 minutes. Spread over chocolate; cool completely. Serve immediately or cover and chill. Let stand at room temperature at least 30 minutes before serving. Yield: 1 (9-inch) cheesecake.

Note: For testing purposes only, we used Smucker's caramel topping.

German Chocolate Cheesecake

*This chocolate lover's dream is all decked out for a party with a crisp
chocolate crust and a frosting adorned with pecans and coconut.*

1 cup chocolate wafer crumbs
   (19 wafers)
2 tablespoons sugar
3 tablespoons butter or
   margarine, melted
3 (8-ounce) packages cream
   cheese, softened
¾ cup sugar
¼ cup unsweetened cocoa

2 teaspoons vanilla extract
3 large eggs
⅓ cup evaporated milk
⅓ cup sugar
¼ cup butter or margarine
1 large egg, lightly beaten
½ teaspoon vanilla extract
½ cup chopped pecans
½ cup flaked coconut

• Stir together first 3 ingredients; press into bottom of a 9-inch
springform pan. Bake at 325° for 10 minutes. Cool.
• Beat cream cheese and next 3 ingredients at medium speed with an
electric mixer until blended. Add eggs, 1 at a time, beating just until
blended after each addition. Pour into prepared crust.
• Bake at 350° for 35 minutes. Gently run a knife around edge of
cheesecake to release sides of pan; cool. Chill 8 hours.
• Stir together evaporated milk and next 4 ingredients in a saucepan.
Cook over medium heat, stirring constantly, 7 minutes. Stir in pecans
and coconut; spread over cheesecake. Yield: 1 (9-inch) cheesecake.

Espresso Cheesecake

This rich cake boasts espresso and chocolate in every bite—the perfect combination for a grand finale.

2½ cups graham cracker crumbs
½ cup plus 2 tablespoons butter
   or margarine, melted
2 teaspoons almond extract
4 (8-ounce) packages cream
   cheese, softened
⅔ cup sugar

3 large eggs
8 (1-ounce) squares semisweet
   chocolate, melted
⅓ cup milk
2 teaspoons instant espresso
   powder
Garnish: chocolate curls

• Combine first 3 ingredients in a medium bowl; stir well. Press mixture into bottom and 2 inches up sides of a 9-inch springform pan. Set aside.
• Beat cream cheese at high speed with an electric mixer until creamy. Gradually add sugar, beating well. Add eggs, 1 at a time, beating after each addition. Add melted chocolate; beat well. Combine milk and espresso powder, stirring until espresso dissolves. Add to cream cheese mixture; beat until smooth. Pour mixture into prepared crust.
• Bake at 350° for 45 to 50 minutes or until center is almost set. Cool to room temperature in pan on a wire rack; cover and chill 8 hours. Gently run a knife around edge of cheesecake to release sides of pan; carefully remove pan. Garnish, if desired. Yield: 1 (9-inch) cheesecake.

Warm Fudge-Filled Cheesecake

Warm leftover cheesecake slices in the microwave 30 seconds before serving.

½ cup butter or margarine,
    softened
⅓ cup sugar
1 cup all-purpose flour
1 tablespoon vanilla, divided
⅔ cup chopped pistachios
4 (8-ounce) packages cream
    cheese, softened

1½ cups sugar
4 large eggs
2 cups (12-ounce package)
    semisweet chocolate
    mini-morsels
Sweetened whipped cream
    (optional)
Garnish: chocolate shavings

• Beat butter at medium speed with an electric mixer until creamy; add ⅓ cup sugar, beating well. Gradually add flour, beating at low speed until blended. Stir in 1 teaspoon vanilla and pistachios. Press into bottom and 1½ inches up sides of a 9-inch springform pan. Bake at 350° for 12 to 15 minutes or until golden. Cool on a wire rack.

• Beat cream cheese at medium speed with an electric mixer until light and fluffy; gradually add 1½ cups sugar, beating well. Add eggs, 1 at a time, beating just until yellow disappears. Stir in remaining 2 teaspoons vanilla. (Do not overmix.)

• Pour half of batter into crust; sprinkle with chocolate morsels to within ¾ inch of edge. Pour in remaining batter, starting at outer edge and working toward center. Place cheesecake on a baking sheet.

• Bake at 350° for 1 hour or until set. Cool on a wire rack 1 hour. Serve slightly warm with sweetened whipped cream, if desired. Garnish, if desired. Yield: 1 (9-inch) cheesecake.

Applause Cheesecake

1 (16-ounce) package pecan shortbread cookies (about 22 cookies)
1 cup pecan halves, coarsely chopped
½ cup firmly packed brown sugar
3 tablespoons orange liqueur, divided
1⅓ cups almond toffee bits
3 (8-ounce) packages cream cheese, softened
1 cup granulated sugar
3 large eggs
½ cup whipping cream
1 tablespoon all-purpose flour
1 tablespoon vanilla extract
1¼ cups semisweet chocolate morsels
¼ cup sour cream
1¼ cups chopped pecans, toasted
½ cup caramel topping

• Position knife blade in food processor bowl; add 22 cookies, reserving others for another use, 1 cup pecans, and brown sugar. Process until finely ground. Add 1 tablespoon liqueur; process until well blended, stopping to scrape down sides. Firmly press crumb mixture into bottom and up sides of a 10-inch springform pan. Sprinkle toffee bits over crust. Set aside.

• Beat cream cheese at medium speed with an electric mixer until creamy; gradually add sugar, beating well. Add eggs, 1 at a time, beating after each addition. Add whipping cream, flour, and vanilla; beat 5 minutes. Pour batter into prepared pan.

• Bake at 325° for 1 hour and 15 minutes or until center is almost set. Cool in pan on a wire rack 15 minutes.

• Combine chocolate morsels and sour cream in a heavy saucepan. Cook over low heat, stirring constantly, until chocolate melts. Spread chocolate mixture evenly over cheesecake. Sprinkle 1¼ cups pecans over chocolate. Combine caramel topping and remaining 2 tablespoons liqueur; spread evenly over pecans. Cool to room temperature in pan on wire rack; cover and chill at least 8 hours. Gently run a knife around edge of cheesecake to release sides of pan; carefully remove pan. Yield: 1 (10-inch) cheesecake.

Note: For testing purposes only, we used Keebler Pecan Shortbread Sandies for pecan shortbread cookies and Grand Marnier for orange liqueur.

Black and White Cheesecake

Big chips of coconut spike the soft whipped cream that covers this cheesecake.

1½ cups shortbread cookie
    crumbs
2 tablespoons granulated sugar
3 tablespoons butter or
    margarine, melted
¾ cup butter or margarine
8 (1-ounce) squares semisweet
    chocolate
1 (8-ounce) package cream
    cheese, softened

1 (3-ounce) package cream
    cheese, softened
½ cup granulated sugar
3 large eggs
⅓ cup cream of coconut
1¼ cups whipping cream
2 tablespoons powdered sugar
½ teaspoon vanilla extract
1 (3-ounce) package coconut
    chips

• Combine first 3 ingredients; stir well. Press into bottom of a greased 9-inch springform pan. Bake at 350° for 10 to 12 minutes or until toasted. Set aside.

• Reduce oven temperature to 300°. Combine ¾ cup butter and chocolate in a heavy saucepan. Cook over medium-low heat until melted, stirring often. Remove from heat, and cool.

• Beat cream cheese at medium speed with an electric mixer until creamy. Add ½ cup granulated sugar; beat well. Add eggs, 1 at a time, beating just until blended after each addition. Stir in cooled chocolate mixture and cream of coconut. Pour into prepared pan. Bake at 300° for 40 minutes or until cheesecake is barely set. Cool to room temperature in pan on a wire rack; cover and chill 8 hours.

• Beat whipping cream at high speed until foamy; gradually add powdered sugar, beating until soft peaks form. Add vanilla; beat just until blended.

• Gently run a knife around edge of cheesecake to release pan; carefully remove pan. Place cheesecake on a serving plate. Frost top and sides with whipped cream mixture. Gently press coconut onto sides, and sprinkle on top of frosted cheesecake. Chill thoroughly. Yield: 1 (9-inch) cheesecake.

Note: For testing purposes only, we used Melissa's Dried Coconut Chips. You can find them near packets of dried fruits in the produce section of grocery stores; you can also buy these wide coconut shavings in stores where nuts are sold in bulk. Or you can substitute flaked coconut.

Chocolate Cookie Cheesecake

2 cups cream-filled chocolate sandwich cookie crumbs (20 cookies)
2 tablespoons butter or margarine, melted
¼ cup firmly packed brown sugar
4 (8-ounce) packages cream cheese, softened
1¼ cups granulated sugar
⅓ cup whipping cream
2 tablespoons all-purpose flour
1 teaspoon vanilla extract
4 large eggs

2 cups coarsely crumbled cream-filled chocolate sandwich cookies (14 cookies)
1 (16-ounce) container sour cream
¼ cup granulated sugar
1 teaspoon vanilla extract
⅓ cup whipping cream
1¼ cups semisweet chocolate morsels
1 teaspoon vanilla extract
Garnish: additional cream-filled chocolate sandwich cookies, coarsely crumbled

• Combine first 3 ingredients in a medium bowl; firmly press mixture evenly into bottom and 2 inches up sides of a lightly greased 10-inch springform pan. Bake at 325° for 12 minutes; set aside.
• Beat cream cheese at medium speed with an electric mixer until creamy. Gradually add 1¼ cups granulated sugar, beating well. Add ⅓ cup whipping cream, flour, and 1 teaspoon vanilla; beat well. Add eggs, 1 at a time, beating after each addition.
• Pour 3½ cups of batter into prepared crust. Top with 2 cups crumbled cookies; pour in remaining batter. Bake at 325° for 1 hour and 15 minutes.
• Combine sour cream, ¼ cup granulated sugar, and 1 teaspoon vanilla; spread over cheesecake. Bake at 325° for 7 minutes. Turn off oven, and leave cheesecake in oven with door closed 45 minutes. Remove cheesecake from oven, and cool completely on a wire rack. Cover and chill 8 hours. Gently run a knife around edge of cheesecake to release sides of pan; carefully remove pan.
• Combine ⅓ cup whipping cream and semisweet chocolate morsels in a saucepan; stir over low heat until chocolate melts. Stir in 1 teaspoon vanilla. Remove from heat. Carefully spread mixture over cheesecake, allowing it to drip down sides. Store cheesecake in refrigerator. Garnish, if desired. Yield: 1 (10-inch) cheesecake.

Note: For testing purposes only, we used Oreo cookies.

Caramel-Brownie Cheesecake

1¾ cups vanilla wafer crumbs
(about 39 wafers)
⅓ cup butter or margarine,
melted
1 (14-ounce) package caramels
1 (5-ounce) can evaporated milk
2½ cups coarsely crumbled
unfrosted brownies
3 (8-ounce) packages cream
cheese, softened

1 cup firmly packed light brown
sugar
3 large eggs
1 (8-ounce) container sour cream
2 teaspoons vanilla extract
Garnishes: whipped cream,
chocolate-lined wafer rolls,
chocolate coffee beans

• Combine vanilla wafer crumbs and butter; firmly press into bottom and 2 inches up sides of a lightly greased 9-inch springform pan. Bake at 350° for 5 minutes. Cool on a wire rack.
• Combine caramels and milk in a small heavy saucepan; cook over low heat, stirring often, until caramels melt. Pour caramel mixture over crust. Sprinkle crumbled brownies over caramel.
• Beat cream cheese at medium speed with an electric mixer 2 minutes or until fluffy. Gradually add brown sugar, mixing well. Add eggs, 1 at a time, beating after each addition just until blended. Stir in sour cream and vanilla.
• Pour batter over brownies in crust. Bake at 350° for 50 minutes to 1 hour or until almost set. Remove from oven; cool to room temperature on a wire rack. Cover and chill at least 4 hours. Gently run a knife around edge of cheesecake to release sides of pan, carefully remove pan. Garnish, if desired. Yield: 1 (9-inch) cheesecake.

Note: Buy prepackaged unfrosted brownies from a bakery, or prepare your favorite mix; cool and crumble enough to yield 2½ cups.

Low-fat Chocolate-Almond Cheesecake

Vegetable cooking spray
¾ cup teddy bear-shaped
    chocolate graham cracker
    cookies, finely crushed
1 (12-ounce) container
    1% low-fat cottage cheese
⅔ cup unsweetened cocoa
⅓ cup all-purpose flour
2 (8-ounce) containers light
    process cream cheese,
    softened

1½ cups sugar
¼ cup amaretto
2 teaspoons vanilla extract
1 large egg
1 egg white
1 cup reduced-calorie frozen
    whipped topping, thawed
2 tablespoons sliced natural
    almonds, lightly toasted

• Coat bottom of a 9-inch springform pan with cooking spray; sprinkle half of crushed cookies into bottom of pan.
• Process cottage cheese in an electric blender 2 to 3 minutes or until very smooth, scraping down sides often; set aside. Sift cocoa and flour together; set aside.
• Beat cream cheese in a large bowl at medium speed with an electric mixer 10 minutes. Gradually add sugar, beating until well blended. Add cottage cheese; beat 1 minute. Add cocoa mixture; beat 1 minute, scraping sides of bowl as needed. Add amaretto and next 3 ingredients; beat 1 minute or until blended. Pour into prepared pan. Bake, uncovered, at 325° for 1 hour and 10 minutes or until set. Remove from oven; sprinkle with remaining half of crushed cookies. Gently run a knife around edge of cheesecake to release sides of pan; cool in pan on a wire rack. Cover and chill at least 8 hours.
• To serve, carefully remove pan; place cheesecake on a serving plate. Pipe or dollop whipped topping around edge, and decorate with almonds. Yield: 1 (9-inch) cheesecake.

Per serving: Calories: 296 (29% from fat); Fat: 9.7g (sat 5.6g, mono 1.2g, poly 0.5g); Protein 9g; Carb 42g; Fiber 2.1g; Chol 41mg; Iron 1.2mg; Sodium 321mg; Calc 112mg

Hot Fudge Cheesecake

This dessert develops a brownielike top as it bakes. Serve any leftover Hot Fudge Sauce over ice cream or pound cake.

1 cup crushed saltine crackers
½ cup finely chopped walnuts
6 tablespoons butter or
   margarine, melted
3 tablespoons sugar
6 (1-ounce) squares semisweet
   chocolate

¾ cup butter or margarine
1 (8-ounce) package cream
   cheese, softened
¾ cup sugar
3 large eggs
Hot Fudge Sauce
Garnish: fresh mint sprigs

• Combine first 4 ingredients; stir well. Firmly press into bottom and 2½ inches up sides of a lightly greased 7-inch springform pan. Bake at 350° for 8 minutes. Set aside.
• Reduce oven temperature to 300°. Combine chocolate squares and ¾ cup butter in a heavy saucepan. Cook over medium-low heat until mixture is melted and smooth, stirring often. Remove from heat, and cool.
• Beat cream cheese at medium speed with an electric mixer until creamy. Add ¾ cup sugar; beat well. Add eggs, 1 at a time, beating after each addition. Stir in cooled chocolate mixture. Pour into prepared crust.
• Bake at 300° for 50 minutes to 1 hour or until almost set. Turn off oven. Let cheesecake cool in oven 30 minutes. Remove to a wire rack; cool to room temperature.
• Gently run a knife around edge of cheesecake to release sides of pan; carefully remove pan. Serve cheesecake with warm Hot Fudge Sauce. Garnish, if desired. Yield: 1 (7-inch) cheesecake.

Hot Fudge Sauce

2 cups (12-ounce package)
   semisweet chocolate
   morsels

1 cup half-and-half
1 tablespoon butter or margarine
1 teaspoon vanilla extract

• Combine chocolate morsels and half-and-half in a heavy saucepan. Cook over medium heat until chocolate melts and mixture is smooth, stirring often. Remove from heat; stir in butter and vanilla. Yield: 2 cups.

Index

*Find these crust recipes as the first step of the cheesecake recipes. You can use these crust recipes for other cheesecakes, but take note of the different sizes of pans that may be involved.